Saber Fencing

for kids:

THAT EVERY PARENT MUST READ

Michael Shender

DEDICATION

To all the English teachers out there, there is no second meaning, there is no hidden motif, there is no overarching theme, and there is no journey leading to enlightenment. It's just an instructional book on how to fence please don't pick it apart.

CONTENTS

ACKNOWLEDGMENTS

I wish to thank coaches Alex Fotiyev, Oleh Tretyak, Alex Kushkov and Dr. Leo Yampolsky for their support and unparalleled wealth of expertise that they so generously share, for their critical and helpful comments on early drafts. I'd like to extend a special thanks to American Fencing Alliance for raising awareness and making fencing a more popular sport among children. AFA Roadmap system printed in this book is compact, clear path for kids to develop fencing skills, leadership qualities and stay involved with fencing. I would like to thank my dad for his optimistic support and silly illustrations. Finally I'd like to thank my sister Nika and my teammates and friends Alan, Zach, and Grant for their friendship and persistent challenge that makes me work harder. I am especially thankful to my mother for introducing me to the sport of fencing and encouraging me every step of my journey.

The Fencing Story

In a land far far away fencing is the most important sport of all.

Fencers gathered from far and wide to compete for glory and medals. This is when young Larry and Robin decided to learn the art of fencing. What they did not realize was not only do fencers have to be strong, courageous and disciplined, but they also follow a strict set of rules written in an ancient language that no one could understand. They searched distant lands to find the best master who could teach them this intricate art. To their dismay they discovered a great number of fencing schools in the  lands near and far. They finally set their sights on a great master who agreed to teach them.

Fencing as active lifestyle

Larry and Robin decided to learn all they could about fencing. They found an old book with pictures of great masters. The book described fencing as a combat skill when your life depended on it. It was necessary to defeat your enemies and protect yourself on the battlefield. The book described attacks with sharp point of the blade and cutting edges, it talked about honor, bravery, and physical fitness necessary to dodge attacks and swing the weapon.

Since then fencing has become a sport primarily concerned with physical fitness and educational aspects. Fencing develops strength, endurance, agility it also develops personal qualities like determination, courage, self-control, perseverance, and sport it fosters proactive quick thinking.

Fencing is motorically complex sport imposing high demands on athletes, but it is possible to master with constant practice. Complexity of fencing unparalleled to any other sport, it requires fencers to use all of the human physical and mental abilities. Fencer must have agility and fast reaction times to outpace opponent offensively or defensively.

Fencer must be astute to maintain balance, precise movements and exact aim with fast changes of positions during a series of unique non-repeating sequences of motion. Fencer must be able to maintain physical performance as well as attention, clarity and sharpness of mind throughout prolonged tournaments. Research shows that fencing has far greater impact on brain development than any other sport. Fencer's brain develops more-compact and fibrous white matter. White matter is what carries signals from one part of the brain to another. More-compact white matter is associated with faster and more efficient nerve activity.

Important Boring Stuff

Gravity, momentum, inertia. You heard about those even if you are from Mars, but if you are from this planet you certainly know what those do.

Gravity

You can be certain that if you jump up you will be brought down by gravity. Important to remember when you practice footwork, the floor is going to be there to catch you.

Momentum and Inertia

I will not bore you with explanation of how these are different. Important point to remember to start motion you need to apply force.

To change direction of movement you need to apply force to stop movement and then apply more force to start movement in a new direction. The same is true for your opponent.

It is important to remember this when practicing, especially when working on cuts, feints, and footwork

Geometry

The shortest distance between two points is a straight line. Moving directly forward or backwards instead of zigzagging covers more ground allowing to reach your opponent or get away. Sharp, fast, straight cuts are the most effective.

Larry and Robin worked tirelessly to perfect their footwork, they slashed and thrusted, but still couldn't win. When sitting at home drinking tea they wondered "we can run faster than everyone in the class, we can jump higher than everyone in the class, we can do more pushups and do other exercises better than everyone in the class, but we can't win.

They were brave enough to ask their master why can't we win? The master responded, "It does not only take physical strength to win a fencing match, but strong knowledge of the rules" He pulled out a dusty book. "This is the guide to fencing written by me and my disciples."

Amazed Robin and Larry stared at the book. Finally there it was fencing explained in the language anyone could understand.

Saber Fencing Simplified

To win all you have to do is hit your opponent before he hits you and stay on the strip.

Robin looked at Larry. They were both stunned with confusion. What exactly does that mean? They both wondered. It can't be this easy, can it?

Saber fencing differs from fencing other weapons, because saber fencers may attack using thrusts as well as cuts with the entire surface of the blade. Saber fencing is exciting, highly maneuverable with fast long movements and filled with fast combat actions. The large target makes defensive actions difficult, this makes fencers want to score using <u>active</u> attacking actions, counter-attacks and fake attacks.

Fencing Strip

Larry and Robin both knew that the strip or piste was a narrow rectangle about six feet wide by about 45 feet long with some lines on it. The strip was for fencing as the court was for basketball players. Lines along the long edges of the strip formed side or lateral boundaries. Lines at the ends of the strip were rear boundaries. "Larry, what are the other lines for?" Asked Robin. Master has told this to Larry earlier. With pride of the knowledge that only he now possessed Larry explained "two lines closest to the middle called En Garde lines. Fencers stand behind those before they start fencing. Space between the En Garde lines is often called the box. Lines closer to back of the strip are warning lines, to tell fencer that they are getting close to the end of the strip."

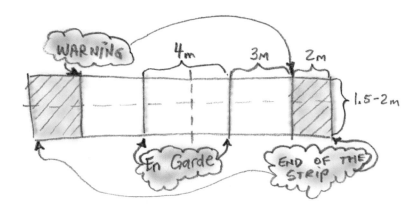

Rules of the Strip

In the event that a fencer's steps off a strip they are considered to have fallen and unable to score a touch. On the other hand a fencer that stays on the strip is allowed to score even if opponent is off the strip. When a fencer steps of the side of a strip the referee will stop fencing. Then fencer who stepped off the strip must move back one meter, about three feet.

RIGHT HANDED STANCE

"Oh, now I understand" said Larry. "You understand that you can't step off the side of the strip, but what happens if you step off the back of the strip?" Robin said. They turned page over. Aha! Fencer is allowed to cross rear boundary, as long as, one foot remains on the strip.

Walk before you run

Larry could run faster than any kid in his class, but he could never beat Robin. As it turns out you can't run or walk when you fence saber.

Crossing feet going forward is prohibited. Crossing occurs when back foot completely passes the front foot. Should this occur fencing is stopped and offender receives a warning - yellow card.

To start moving forward one must first enter the en gard position. Leading foot in front and other leg behind, with heels on the same line, forming an L-shape. With knees slightly bent. Keep your feet about one and a half of your foot length apart.

Now you can begin moving forwards or backwards. To move forward move your front leg forward, landing on your heel, then follow it with your back leg. Both legs must move the same distance.

Now to move backwards you must perform the same action but in reverse. This time you lead with the back leg and follow with the front leg.

Step forward is called ADVANCE, step back is called RETREAT. Other fencing steps are LUNGE, APEL, BALESTRA and Flunge were mentioned, but not described. While Robin looked puzzled, impatient Larry thumbed through the book found the entire chapter on footwork a little further.

Another rule stated that a left handed fencer should always be placed to the left of the referee when facing a right handed opponent.

FOOTWORK

Footwork is foundation of fencing. Good footwork allows fencer to rapidly accelerate, perform sharp stops, and immediate changes in direction. Most importantly good footwork allows fencer to stay in balance.

En Garde

This is the starting position, ballet third position is derived from fencing En Garde. To establish the En Garde position fencers place their front foot (right foot if right handed, left if left handed) directly behind the En Garde line. Front foot if positioned along the length of the strip. Heel of the fencers back foot is placed directly behind of the front foot heel. Feet positioned at 90^0 to each other, if brought together they would form an L shape. Move your back foot about one and a half of your foot size back.

After the your feet are in position, next you have to square your shoulders to face forward. Place your saber in parry #3 position and bend your knees.
Vous Voilà!

Advance

In other words this is a step forward that can be performed in variety of shapes and sizes. Short, long, slow, and fast. Advance starts with a movement of your <u>front foot forward</u>, landing it on the <u>heel</u>. After landing your front foot finish advance with a step forward with your back foot fencers can vary size of the advance to create a broken rhythm and to catch opponent off guard. Sometime a series of a super short advances

(almost in place) are used to prepare an attack while maintaining the right of way.

For instance you could start your attack with a few short advances and finish the attack with a couple large fast advances.

Retreat

It is arguably the most important skill to master. Anyone can move forward faster than backwards. Human beings were designed to walk forwards, but not backwards. As a result it is very difficult to master rapid movements backwards.

Retreat is completed by reaching back with back leg (left leg for right handed fencers and right leg if fencer is a lefty). After you place back leg down, you finish the retreat by bringing your front leg back the same distance your back leg moved. retreats can vary in size and speed.

Jump Back

Some time you must perform a very large rapid retreat by jumping back. In this case you start by slightly elevating your back leg then rapidly throwing it further back, followed by a strong push of the front leg, landing both feet simultaneously. Jump back style retreat is often used to perform a fake attack. It is important to be able to make a series of rapid steps back. People usually lose balance after one or two rapid retreats, therefore make three, four or even more fast retreats combination a part of your every practice and warm up routine.

Lunge

A lunge is used to end the attack. Lunge can vary in length depending on how far away his opponent and if the opponent is standing still, moving toward you or away from you.

To lunge from the En Garde position a fencer elevates his front foot toes, move your foot forward skimming the floor surface, push off with the back foot pushing forward, then rapidly extend your hand forward and <u>land the front foot on the heel</u>. It is important to check your position at the end of the lunge when practicing.

Lets look at the lunge a little closer. As the advance, lunge can vary in size. The timing for hand movement can be slightly different as well. In one case you realize that opponent is too close and a quick short lunge is needed to finish your attack spontaneously with a rapid hand extension. In another case your opponent remained far and a larger lunge with a strong push from your back leg is needed to reach the target.

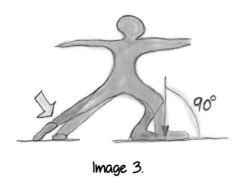

Image 3.

After a proper lunge the <u>back foot remains flat</u> on the ground, back leg is straight, front leg is bent with thigh almost parallel to the floor. It is important that front leg knee does not pass over front heel. In other words <u>angle formed by front leg should not be less than 90°.</u>

Lunge Exercises

Quarter Game

There are several ways to develop a good lunge. The Quarter game is one of the most effective exercises to develop correct lunge technique. To play, simply place a quarter on the ground, step on it with your heel or front foot. in a comfortable En Garde position. Lift the toes of your front foot and lunge pushing the quarter forward with the heel. This game will ensure that front foot is moving parallel to the floor and most importantly landing on its heel.

Agility Ladder Exercise

For next routine you will need the agility ladder. Lay out the agility ladder on the floor. Sit En Garde position on one side of the ladder with toes of your front foot against the ladder's edge. Make a half step inside the ladder placing your front foot on the heel inside the square, than lunge over the ladder. Move sideways to face next square and repeat. By making half step with heel positions the fencer in wider stance with toes of the front foot pointing up. Biomechanics of this position prevents a common mistake of overloading the front foot and ensuring that final <u>lunge lands on the heel</u>.

Balestra

It is also known as a jump step is a very useful technique for keeping balance in the long attack and finishing your attack. It can be performed in place or with a motion forward. The Balestra is performed by a jump while kicking forward with a front foot and landing both feet together. It may sound funny, but it is a very effective when used to change the rhythm or make explosive rapid attack. There are several biomechanical principles at work with balestra. During advance most of the time fencers are off balance, because they are standing on one leg. There is a brief moment between steps when both feet are on the ground. Even then momentum keeps the body off balance. When fencers land after a jump, both feet are firmly planted on the ground, knees are bent and body is in balance this creates a strong foundation for a fast lunge or advance lunge. At the same time balestra is a startling move. Your opponent may get scared and run away. Don't worry they can't run too far, but moving further forward unopposed allows you to push your opponent closer to the rear boundary, limiting their options.

Appel

Stomping your foot on the ground is called an Appel. The action looks very similar to an incomplete step forward or a half advance. An appel is very simple to perform and is useful when performing fake attacks or setting up counterattack in preparation. For a fake attack you should practice combination of a slow advance, sharp appel, retreat or jump back. Counter attack should start exactly the same way with a slower and softer appel, only replacing jump back with lunge. Fake attack may be easier for beginners. Sometimes appell is used to stop the bout. In this instance fencer should raise ungloved hand and stomp back foot several times to attract attention of the referee.

Flunge

This move is a cross breed of fleche and lunge or just a flying lunge. Since crossing feet going forward is not allowed in saber, running attack  (fleche - still used in slower foil and epee) was replaced by a rapid flying attack.

The flange is an advanced step that requires very good balance.. It heavily reliant on core strength and strong legs. Arguably flunge can be even faster than fleche. It is performed by pushing off the front foot rather than back one. Keep in mind fencer that flunges in the box will lose against an opponent performing a regular lunge.. DON'T FLUNGE IN THE BOX. Flunge is an athletic move, failed flunge is almost unrecoverable. Other elements must be perfected before attempting a flunge.

Target area

The valid saber target area includes Head, neck, shoulders, arms above wrists, and body above the line connecting hip bones.

Areas colored red represent valid target area for saber fencers.

Saber Valid Target Area

Although the non-weapon hand is the only unprotected area of a fencer's body, with proper technique the fencer's hand is completely out of your opponent's reach.

Saber - traditionally a cavalry weapon was used while on horseback. In the fight it was considered ill-mannered to injure a defenseless animal thus limiting target to rider above the saddle.

We can only assume that in those days horses were held in the higher esteem than people riding them.

Saber and How to hold it

Saber Parts

Saber consists of the following required parts:

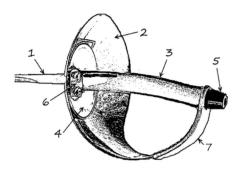

1. Blade
2. Guard
3. Grip
4. Pad
5. Pommel
6. Socket
7. Insulating Sleeve

It is important to note that most of the saber parts are interchangeable for left and right handed fencers except for the guard. Right handed guard is wider on the right, left handed guard is its mirror image. Socket is installed on the side of the thinner side of the guard.

Holding the saber

To hold the saber place thumb over flat area at the top of the grip about half an inch away from the guard, then wrap fingers loosely around the grip.

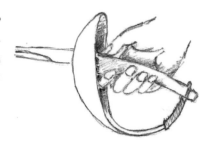

By rotating the wrist and squeezing the grip fencer can perform a number of feints and cuts.

Who scored the touch?

If no rules has been broken and only red light is lit on the scoring box, fencer on the left wins the touch. If there is only green light lit, fencer on the right wins.

If both red and green lights are on the fencer who has the attack wins. Director decides who had the attack. If both fencers performed identical attacks in the box nobody scores.

When a valid target (anything above the waste except wrists) is touched by saber the scoring machine turn on a red light for Left and green light for right touch. If both fencers hit simultaneously, both red and green lights are on. If one fencer hits just a little bit faster than the other only one light will be on. Second touch will be blocked by the machine. How much is a little bit? Scoring boxes are timed to block touches that are 1/20 - 1/25 of a second apart. A little less time than it takes to sneeze.

OH, COOL
WHO IS YOUR MASTER?

The ATTACK mystery

The Word attack has two meanings in fencing. It means priority or a right of way when we talk about who scored. It is also used to describe a type of action or a plan. You will hear names like Quick Attack or Fake Attack.

Attack a.k.a. right of way

Having the attack is the most important aspect of scoring points in fencing. Although scoring points on the attack may seem like a simple task, but there are several ways to lose or gain the attack.

To understand if you have the attack, you need to see what you are doing in relation to the other fencer. One thing is certain you can't get an attack by standing still. To get an attack you must move forward while extending arm toward the target.

Larry and Robin got on the strip and after command fence stated to charge each other over and over, soon they both got exhausted, neither one of them earned a single point. They wondered why they both received zero points, when two fencers perform the same action <u>in the box</u> no point is awarded.

Stop

Stop moving forward or move back and your attack is over. Fortunately same is true for your opponent.

Parry

Parry is to block the opponent's hit with your sword. You regain the attack after the parry by starting your own attack. If you stop or continue moving back you will allow your opponent to start another attack. On the attack it is important to look-out for the opponent's parry by using feints to confuse your opponent where you are going to hit.

Beat

Beat by using your blade to strike the top 3/4rs of your opponent's blade, you regain the attack. While on the offence it is important to look-out for opponents beats and protect your blade from your opponent beats.

Distance Parry

Distance parry is a big name for a dodge. Dodging your opponents hit is an effective way to regain the attack. It is important for attacker to finish the attack unpredictably to ensure hitting the opponent before they dodge. Simply, swing and miss the target and your attack is over.

Intricately detailed guards were designed to let fencer break opponent's blade, by catching it in one of the hooks or other openings during the parry.

Riposte

A riposte is an offensive action in response to the opponent's failed attack. For example Robin starts her attack after Larry falls short, missing his attack. Riposte can be short or immediate, or long that requires a number of steps to reach retreating opponent. In short riposte is another name for attack.

Best defense is good offence

Of every 10 points 8 are scored on the attack. You can dodge and parry all day long, but to score you need to hit the target. Remember, you get no points for hitting opponents sword. You may get a point only if you hit your opponent. You may be friends off the strip, but on the strip you are competitors. Your competitor has given you permission to hit and will no doubt will not hesitate to hit you to score.

Plan

Most seasoned fencers create a plan before the get En Garde. They decide what action they will perform and what they will do if it fails. Sometimes the plan may 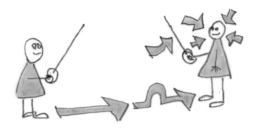 have to be revised in action. It is too late to make a plan after the fence command.

For beginner and intermediate fencers plan mainly consists of deciding what type of attack to perform. Quick, long or fake.

Quick Attack

  Attack in the box that consists of one or two steps forward and a lunge. This is probable a most frequently performed action. Frequently quick attacks result in no points awarded to either side. Crazy?! Why waste time and energy on something that gives no points? While it is true that a great

23

number of quick attacks result in no points, it is still one of the most important skills to master. I'm sure, there are wizards in many kingdoms that wrote books on the value of quick attacks alone.

Well performed quick attack can result in a win, but also it can set the stage to make fake or long attack more successful.

Quick attack is an effective way to score if your opponent has decided to perform a long attack.

It is a good idea to be prepared for opponents fake attack when your plan is quick attack. Possible remedies against this crafty move may be: second intention counter-attack, parry, or converting quick attack into a long attack.

Long Attack

OFFENCE   DEFENCE

An attack requiring multiple steps to chase an opponent that is moving back. It is recommended to use feints to confuse your opponent at the end of this attack. Long attack may require a number of slow preparation steps, several fast steps and a lunge.

Long attack may be your initial plan if you anticipate for opponent to move back. Long attack may also be required after a successful fake attack or opponent's failed attack.

Fake Attack

This type of attack is not an attack at all. Fake attack is an intentional surrender of an attack with such pizzazz and theatrics that forces your opponent to believe that you are performing a quick attack. If performed correctly your opponent will end an attack too soon and fall short. As result you regain an attack and advantage over an off-balance opponent.

How to perform these attacks and some useful tips will be discussed after the footwork section.

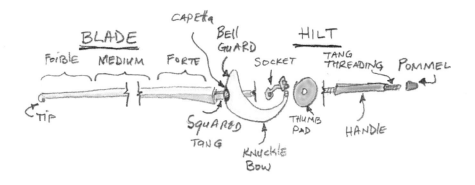

Saber Deconstructed

To Parry or not to Parry

Often it is important to be able to block a hit this is a time for a parry.

Distance Parry

Best parry is simply not being there. Jumpback to dodge opponent's blade and you successfully get the attack by evading your opponent's blade. There are ways that would make performing this parry easier.

Don't guess, know

You must know, not guess the time when to move. It would be easy if you could read minds or see the future. How would you know when opponent going to hit, without a mind reading ability? The answer is simple. MAKE THEM DO IT when you want it. Larry and Robby looked at each other confused. How? Just like a fake attack, fake counter-attack will do the same trick and force your opponent to swing at you.

By now you should begin to see the light at the end of a tunnel. Fencing is not reactive, it is proactive. You must force opponents to play your game, to be where you want them to be and do what you want them to do.

Other popular saber parries are 3, 4, 5, and 2. These parries are used to block attacks using the blade. It is important to know and remember parry numbers, so you can follow your fencing master instructions. Keep in mind the number represents what you are going to protect. For example parry #3 means that you block your side of the arm holding saber, not your right side, as it is different for righties and lefties.

When learning perries remember X is better than II.

What to Block not Where to Block

Parry #3

Protects body on the side of the hand holding the saber. Saber points straight up in the air. Guard position is low at waist level. Body and hands are in the En Garde position. During the parry wrist of the hand holding the saber pronates outward with a closing motion.

Parry #4

Protects body on the side opposite of the hand with saber. Saber points straight up in the air. Guard low, in front at waist level at 7 o'clock. During the parry wrist of the hand holding the saber pronates inward with a closing motion.

27

Parry #5

Protects head and shoulders. From En Garde raise saber guard directly above your head holding saber across with a point slightly higher and forward. Elbow should not be outside of the vertical line protected by guard.

Parry #2

Used to block attacks under arm, cuts and thrusts to the lower torso. From En Garde position point saber down. It is perhaps a more advanced move and not necessary for beginner fencers.

Circle Parries

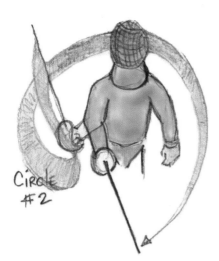

Circle #2

Protect multiple sectors with a windshield wiper like, sweeping motion. Circle parries are very effective defense tool. During the circle parry point of the saber is moving in a semicircle spiral like fashion. End position of the blade determines parry number. For example if you start in the En Garde position and during the parry rotate tip of the saber forward then around drawing an inward spiral ending with blade down in the parry #2 position this would make a circle parry 2. In saber Circle Parry 3 is probably the most functional. Opposite of parry #2 it starts at parry #2 and finish at parry #3.

Parry, when and how

Saber parry can be done with motion forward, at a full stop or moving back. There is a reason for each type of action. Usually, beginners are taught to take a parry with a step back. This strategy allows more room for error and so is more successful at early stages. Taking parry at full stop or moving forward requires additional setup and preparation. These strategies become viable over time, as fencer develops sense of distance and timing of the action. All motions need to be timed. There is such thing as too fast. <u>Sometimes fencer must move slowly to prepare the action.</u>

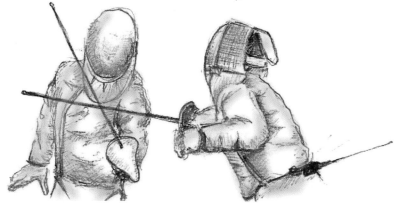

Left handed fencer (blue) parry #4 attack of the right handed fencer (red). Keep in mind the same cut would be called cut to 4 against a lefty and cut to 3 if fencing a righty.

It is advisable to provoke your opponent to hit. This makes opponent's hit less prepared, more predictable and so, easier to parry. There are many ways to provoke your opponent. Fake counterattack, search your opponent's blade for a beat, a small jump forward, or simply stop and wait. All these will do the trick. Keep in mind that your plan is to move back immediately and take a parry.

Known is good, unknown not so much

It is easy to walk with your eyes open. You can easily avoid obstacles and navigate complex path. With your eyes closed even simple tasks like walking become far more difficult. Cooking with closed eyes is hazardous at best. Crossing street without looking is deadly.

What do we know?

- We know that attackers are looking for an opportunity to finish the attack with a cut or a thrust, as soon as, you give them an opening.
- We know that your opponent's saber is the same length as yours.
- We know that attackers will not attempt to hit when they are too far.
- We know that attackers needs to continuously move forward.
- We know if our opponent is right handed or left handed.
- We know that attackers feel confident when you are almost off the strip and unable to move further back.
- We know that holding your saber with the tip pointing forward will make it more challenging for attacker to get close.
- We know that the shortest distance between two points is a straight line.
- We know that a taller opponent is more likely to hit upper regions, head and shoulders
- We know that a shorter opponent is more likely to hit lower regions, under arm, and to thrust.
- We know the current position of opponent's saber.

- We know where previous attacks landed, also we know what actions this opponent favors by observing other bouts.
- We may also know what actions the referee may favor.

Only knowledge relevant to the current bout is useful knowledge.

- We also know if it's warm or cold outside, if you have unfinished homework, if somebody is screaming on the adjacent strip, if your parents are watching, where you will go for dinner and what you will eat, $E=MC^2$ and so on. This is not useful in the bout therefore ignore it.

Using the useful knowledge we can formulate a defense strategy. You know that attacker needs to finish the attack, even with two light on the attacker wins. If attackers see a counterattack coming they will attempt to hit as quick as possible to score. This is why using a fake counter attack is a good tool. Now that you successfully provoked your opponent to finish their attack prematurely, you must decide what parry to take and how. When attacker believes that a counter attack is imminent, they don't have time for complex blade movements and are forced to finish the attack quickly to a sector where the blade was pointing at the time of the counterattack.

With a shorter opponent you may choose to take a distance parry. With distance parry the attackers will miss no matter where they try to hit. So, immediately following the fake counterattack you must jump back and may be take one additional step back to dodge the attack you just provoked. It is a good idea to take a parry while you jumping back. It will protect you if you did not move far enough, also by moving your hand back you remove more target as well. For beginners I think parry #3 or circle parry #3 are good ideas.

If your opponent has the tip of the saber up, following a fake counterattack you may choose to jump back and take parry #5. More advanced fencers may choose to step forward following a fake counterattack and take parry #5 with a rapid riposte. This move, if done properly, limits when and where your opponent can hit so severely that they will have hard time avoiding your parry. Parry #2 or #3 are smart choices if the attacker's blade is pointing down.

Searches and Invitations

Other Ways to provoke attackers are searches and invitations.

Search

If you choose to beat the attackers blade to gain the attack. You must rotate your saber in a circular motion to find the attackers blade. <u>Not every search is successful</u> and usually presents opportunity for attacker to score. Knowing

that, you may use the search as provocation and immediately cover exposed area. using the same strategy as before you may take parry #3 or #5 if attacker's blade is up or parry #3 or #2 if attacker's blade is down.

Invitation

Simply open what you want your opponent to hit and then parry the attack to that area. For example you may move your saber to a position in the middle exposing your hand, then take parry #3 if attacker takes the bait. Keep in mind, smart attacker will pretend to fall into your trap and will <u>faint</u> (fake) to your exposed area then hit a different location. In this case an attacker might faint 3 then attack 4. This is why you need to perfect timing and style of invitations.

All these tricks will not work every time, but they will improve your odds. For example if you decide to hold parry #5 you will be exposing 3 and 4. When opponent makes a cut you would simply guess and take parry #4. Your odds of success are 50/50. If you score on every two out of three of your attacks and your defensive game is 50/50 you win the bout, but you can do even better.

Stop guessing. Anticipate

If you stop guessing and anticipate the attack you improve your odds substantially. You start by counting how many times your opponents attacks 3, 4 and 5. Then they will not be able to resist when you invite to attack their favorite spot. You should be able to easily parry anticipated attack.

Don't take parry early

Opponent can see an early parry and change the direction of the attack. On the other hand if you

see your opponent is ready to strike you can perform an invitation and take a fake parry just a bit early, exposing where you want them to hit, then move to actual parry. Outsmarting your opponent is one of the most enjoyable parts of the game.

The ancient question of TIME and SPACE

By now your head is spinning trying to visualize all this parry stuff. It is filled with questions of where do I stand and how do I move. I will be honest reading this book may give you a better understanding of fencing, but you would have to buy fairy dust that instantaneously makes you a wonder fencer from another merchant.

You have to practice, practice, practice and when you're done practicing, practice some more to become good at anything.

35

All these techniques will work perfectly only after you master timing and distance. It is very important to understand the distance between you and your opponent that is needed to successfully trick them into believing your counterattack is real.. At the same time you have to gauge how far you have to be to get clear of his attack once it comes. You need to develop body language and theatrics that make your fake intentions convincing.

Use parry to set up a counterattack

Moving your hand into a parry position can be used to prepare a counterattack. The attacker may get confused and hesitate just a tat, if you suddenly take several parries. This may create an opening for a counterattack. For example rapidly take parry #4 then #5, counterattack to your opponent's 3 (forearm) and jump back taking parry #3 or #5.

COMPETITIVE FENCING

ATTACK

The fencing rule book defines an attack as: "The initial offensive action made by extending the arm and continuously threatening the opponent's target ..."

This is vague and hard to explain definition. Many referees are confused by it and their interpretations differ from one to the other. It is important to remember that directors are human, they do their best to interpret fast-paced actions, usually without video replay at their disposal.

Attack in the box

It is important to highlight one attack scenario in particular. It is probably the most frequently performed action in saber fencing. Attack in the box occurs immediately after the "fence" command is given. Both fencers charge forward and touch valid target at the same time, both lights register on the machine. And yet one fencer wins and the other loses.

A few elements to which fencers should pay particular attention to:

1. Footwork

    Many referees will look for aggressive footwork with constant motion forward and ending attack with a lunge.

    If footwork of both fencers is symmetrical call may be made based on blade and hand motion.

2. Hand motion

if both fencers had symmetrical footwork, the fencer who begins hand extension first while IN DISTANCE wins over a fencer who hesitates. Extension of hand out of distance will result in a loss of the attack. Many define right distance or IN DISTANCE as close enough to reach your opponent with lunge or in one step with hand extension.

3. Blade position

If footwork and hand position are the same blade position decides the attack. Blade pointing forward towards the target wins over a blade pointing away from it. Be careful not to swing during the final cut as it can change direction of the blade to point away from the target causing loss of the attack.

4. Line of attack

Lastly, fencer who perform straight attack in one line win over the fencers who perform feints or searches before the final cut.

5. Director

Pay particular attention to actions favored by the director. As you understand by now all fencing actions are scored based on the rule interpreted by a human. There is a small problem with humans. They are all a different. Different vision, reaction, vantage point, personal fencing background, endurance and other factors can affect director's calls. If you disagree with a call, POLITELY ask why this call was made and listen carefully. Referees will look for footwork, blade position, hand extension, and line of the attack. Adjust your game according to the referees previous calls

Attack in the box can be done with a single advance and lunge or a double advance and lunge. Size of the advance and lunge can vary to outplay your opponent. You can make your opponent to hesitate or to end attack too soon. For example single Large or medium size advance followed by a rapid short lunge may catch your opponent in preparation.

Long Attack with Feints

Attacks that have multiple steps to reach your opponent are referred to as long attacks. Attack with multiple movements of the blade, beats and fents is called a composite attack. To perform an effective long attack you should make several blade motions paired with complex footwork.

Although There are an infinite number of combinations of footwork and blade movements when performing a long attack it is important to split the attack into two parts; slow preparation and a fast finish. Let's consider a common long attack, triple advance, double advance ballestra lunge. The preparation would be the triple advance and should be performed slowly. Next comes the explosive finish with a double advance balestra, lunge. Lastly do not forgot to include feints throughout the long attack and when finishing. Beginner fencer should pick a target during the preparatory phase, this will remove hesitation when finishing.

Fake Attack

Fake attack is also called an in and out. To perform this action you must first give up the attack first in such a way that opponent is likely to fail immediately after.

I know it's a bit confusing. Let's clarify. Both fencers perform simultaneous attacks in the box one after another, with no points scored. Larry decides to trick Robin into believing that he is going

to do another quick attack in the box, but instead he stops sharply and moves back as Robin completes her advance and lunge attack falling short and missing the target. Now after Robin failed her attack Larry has regained the attack and an opportunity to score a riposte on Robin who is not able to move back immediately after the lunge.

Larry decided to do a fake attack and Robin committed perform quick attack. Larry sharply changed direction when fooled Robin lunged too early.

to

Robin lost her attack after she fell short and missed. Larry started moving forward preparing his attack.

Tournament First Timers

Larry and Robin decided to go to a tournament, but they knew very little about them. They were very worried that they were not prepared. They had a lot of questions about what equipment they need, where to report, and how the score is kept?

What to bring checklist

Rules require that fencers must have the following items:

- Tall Socks (covering any part of the leg not covered by pants)
- Knickers (fencing pants)
- Underarm protector (½ jacket)
- Fencing Jacket
- Plastic chest protector
          (Optional for men, mandatory for female fencers)
- Saber Mask
- Lame
- Saber glove
- 2 body cords
- 2 mask cords
- 2 sabers

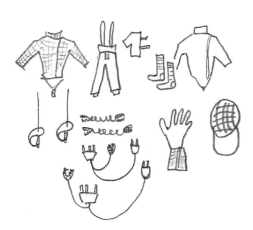

Equipment Inspection

At larger tournaments your equipment may require to pass inspection. Inspectors will check your equipment and mark it with inspection marks, that will be checked later by directors

Visual inspection

Inspector or the bout director will see that your equipment has no holes, cracks or tears. Your mask may be subjected to a punch test to make sure it is safe. Time-to-time you should inspect your own equipment yourself.

Electric Equipment Testing

Electric testing is performed for all electric equipment usually with the exception of the saber. Lame, glove, and mask are tested and marked with stamps. All cords are also tested and marked with colored tape. Tape from prior inspections should be removed after each tournament. Make sure inspection tape.

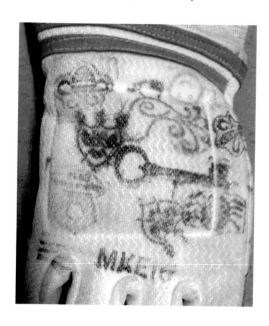

Individual Tournament

In a tournament with many people, fencers are separated in groups called pools of five to seven fencers. They fence five touch bouts with everyone in their pool. Based on the results of pool bouts fencers are seeded into a direct elimination table. They fence Direct Elimination (DE) bouts until only the winner remains.

For example a pool table may look something like this:

POOL 1

	Fencer	1	2	3		VI	TS	TR	TI	Place
1	Larry		V	4		1	9	7	2	1
2	Robin	2		V		1	7	6	1	2
3	Jim	V	1			1	6	9	-3	3

1 vs 2 1-YC CROSSED	2 vs 3	1 vs 3

Translation

Victory Indicator - VI
VI - primary and the most important performance measure.
Victory Indicator shows a number of bouts won by fencer in the pool round.

TS - Touches Scored (add all points in the fencer's row)
TR - Touches Received (add all points in the fencers column)

Touch Indicator - TI

TI - is secondary, but also an extremely important measure. Touch Indicator is calculated by subtracting TR from TS i.e. touches scored minus touches received. It is used as a tiebreaker for fencers with equal number of victories.

V - Victory or roman numeral five

Pool bouts are fenced to 5 touches, so V = 5 points. In some cases one can win with less than 5 points. For example, to record a victory with 3 points scored the director would write V3, this can occur when fencers run out of time in a bout.

If victories are tied, TI determines place.
Below the table usually there is a bout order. Director will cross out bouts that already took place and must record any violations on the score sheet. You can see that fencer 1 (Larry) received a Yellow Card for crossing.

Ordinarily six fencers would not be split in two pools. To illustrate a tournament with multiple pools, we split competitors into two pools of three.

POOL 2

	Fencer	1	2	3	VI	TS	TR	TI	Place
1	Mims		1	4	0	5	10	-5	3
2	Nia	V		V	2	10	2	8	1
3	Sammy	V	2		1	7	9	-2	2

Seeding After Pools

Place	Fencer	VI	TI
1	Nia	2	8
2	Larry	1	2
3	Robin	1	1
4	Sammy	1	-2
5	Jim	1	-3
6	Mims	0	-5
7	-		
8	-		

DE Tableau

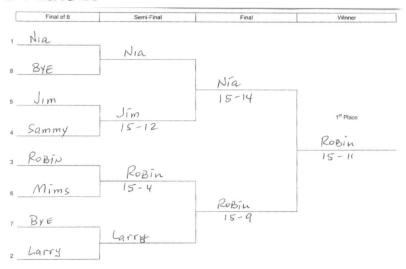

Final of 8	Semi-Final	Final	Winner

1 — Nia

Nia

8 — BYE

Nia
15-14

5 — Jim

Jim
15-12

4 — Sammy

1st Place

Robin
15-11

3 — Robin

Robin
15-4

6 — Mims

Robin
15-9

7 — Bye

Larry

2 — Larry

Who is Bye?

DE table is filled to make an even number of fencers based on the following progression 2, 4, 8, 16, 32, 64 ... Fencers are placed in the DE Tableau as follows: First vs Last, Second vs. Second to Last, etc. In this case 1 and 2 have nobody to fence in 7th and 8th places. 1 and 2 get a <u>Bye</u> and advance to the next round unopposed.

Bout score is recorded under the winner's name.

Final results

Place	Fencer
1	Robin
2	Nia
3T	Larry
3T	Jim
5	Sammy
6	Mims

Robin won 1st place defeating Nia with score 15-11 in the final bout.

Larry and Jim are tied for 3rd place, because there was no fence-off for third in this tournament.

Tournament format is important.
This tournament had 100% promotion to DE after pools. Some of the larger tournaments have 80% promotion to DE. This means that only top 80% of fencers will advance to DE round.

Oops?!

Team Match

Team matches are usually fenced as a relay to 45 touches.
Strongest fencers usually anchor the relay.

Team A						Team B		
1	Robin			vs		Mims		4
2	Larry					Nia		5
3	Jim					Sammy		6
#	Fencer	Touches	Score		Score	Touches	Fencer	#
3	Jim	5	5		1	1	Sammy	6
1	Robin	5	10		9	8	Nia	5
2	Larry	5	15		11	2	Mims	4
1	Robin	5	20		14	3	Sammy	6
3	Jim	5	25		14	0	Mims	4
2	Larry	5	30		28	14	Nia	5
1	Robin	5	35		31	3	Mims	4
2	Larry	5	40		33	2	Sammy	6
3	Jim	3	43		45	12	Nia	5
Penalties			Final Score		Final Score	Penalties		
3 - YC crossing 3 - RC disobedience			43		45	4 - YC turning during bout		

Penalties

Fencer receives penalties for breaking rules. There are four penalties.

1. Ground penalty

This penalty is assessed if fencer steps off the strip during fencing. Penalized fencer must move back one meter.

2. Yellow card

This penalty is given to the fencer for <u>first offence</u>. No points awarded to opponent, but a touch is annulled (does not count). This penalty may result in a loss of a point if both fencers hit.

0 - 0

For example Larry is performing attack and Robin counterattacks at the same time. Larry crossed his feet as both fencers hit. With both lights on Larry receives a yellow card. Larry's touch is annulled while Robin's touch is good. Robin wins this point.

Spectators and coaches can also receive a yellow card as warning for disturbances. For them second offence results in the black card.

3. Red Card

This penalty is given if offence is severe or for every subsequent yellow card offence. For example Larry receives a yellow card for crossing feet, every time he crosses his feet again, in the same bout, he will receive a red card.

If no penalties of any kind are given and Larry receives a yellow or red card, then every penalty that would otherwise resulted in a yellow card will cause a red card and a point awarded to his opponent. Using earlier example Larry receives yellow card for crossing feet during attack as Robin counterattacks. Score is 1 - Robin, 0 - Larry.

The same thing happens again. Larry receives a red card. Robin get two points. One for the valid touch and another for Larry's red card. Score now is 3 - Robin, 0 - Larry.
After command fence during his first step Larry crosses feet going forward. Fencers do not yet hit. Halt, Larry receives a red card and the sore becomes 4 - Robin, 0 - Larry.

4. Black Card

This is the most severe form of punishment. This card is given mostly for disciplinary offences and cheating, offenders are disqualified from the competition. Spectators and coaches can also receive the black card.

Another way to look at penalties is by group. There are four groups of penalties:

Penalty Groups

- 1st Group
  Generally offences on this group penalized with yellow card for first offence.

- 2nd Group
  Offences in this group are penalized with red card.

- 3rd Group
  Fencer will get a red card for first offence in this group and a black card for second offence.

- 4th Group
  Black card is given for all offences in this group.

Complete list of penalties can be found online, but here is a list of a few easily avoidable penalties.

Offence	1st	2nd	3rd
Fencer not present	1st Call	2nd Call	3rd Call
Turning the back to the opponent			
Touching electrical equipment			
Covering target			
Disobeying the referee			
Taking mask off before Halt			
Using non-weapon arm or hand			
Disturbing order on the strip			
Deliberate Brutality			

Mind over matter

Paralyzed by fear, bundle of nerves, heart skipped a beat, butterflies in your stomach are all performance killing effects of your brain's chemistry. People are hardwired to experience fear as self-preservation safeguard that stops us from doing something dangerous. Everybody gets nervous and scared. Good news! There are ways to get less nervous.

Another important point to consider is that people have limits on how fast they run, how high they jump, and how much information they can process in a second. It turns out we can process huge amounts of data very fast. Our eyes, ears, nose, hands, feet can constantly capture data. We also have amazing capability for parallel processing, like walking and chewing bubble gum at the same time, but everything has its limits. Every added simultaneous task slows other processes down. We would have a harder time doing math while watching TV and running on a treadmill. Focusing on one task is a skill.

A good fencer is able to tune out all outside noise and focus on the bout.

Kill the fear

So, first of all, let me assert my firm belief that the only thing we have to fear is fear itself — nameless, unreasoning, unjustified terror which paralyzes needed efforts to convert retreat into advance.

Franklin D. Roosevelt

Beginner's luck is a paradigm that occurs due to a very low initial expectations. First timers usually score points and sometimes even win bouts because they are less afraid to loose. Often you can clearly see a moment when fencer becomes tense and movements become jagged and slow, as fear of loss overloads the brain.

Is it even possible to change natural brain chemistry and body response? Simple answer is YES.

There are many things you can do to avoid and manage fear before and during tournaments. The following are few of them:

1. Routine
2. Physical exercise
3. Ritual
4. Visualization

Routine

Development of a good routine helps to reduce chaos and remain focused on the task. Create a checklist and agenda of what you need to bring, where you need to be and what times. The night before, lay out clothing you will wear the following day, in order of what goes on last on the bottom and first on the top. Decide where you go for breakfast and what you will have. This sounds excessive, but it removes uncertainty and unnecessary stress from what is already stressful day.

Make sure there is time to warm up, stretch, dress and fence warm up bouts.

Sample checklist may be as follows:

☐	Chest protector	6:30 am	Wake up
☐	Plastron	7:00 am	Breakfast place, pancakes
☐	Socks	8:00 am	Equipment check
☐	Knickers	8:20 am	Buy saber
☐	Jacket	8:30 am	Check-in
☐	Lame	9:00 am	Warm-up
☐	Glove	9:15 am	Dress
☐	Mask	9:20 am	Fence warm-up bouts
☐	Sneakers	9:40 am	Visualization
☐	Sabers	9:45 am	Check-in Closed, find your strip
☐	Body Cords	9:50 am	At your strip with equipment
☐	Mask Cords		ready to win
☐	Head phones		
☐	Phone		
☐	Snack		
☐	Journal		
☐	Passport or ID		

Physical exercise

It makes people happy, because physical exercise induces the release of endorphins. Endorphins are chemicals that promote happiness. Your warm-up routine has to be intensive enough to wake up your muscles and release endorphins, yet leave enough energy for competition. Make sure you approach your warm-up routine systematically. You may choose to use the following template for your top to bottom warm up:

All exercises should start slow, gradually increasing range of motion. Consider doing ten repetitions or so for each one of the points below.

1. Tune out distractions with the up-tempo music.
2. Start with walking, slowly increasing pace.
3. As you walk, slow circles with your head clockwise and counterclockwise.
4. Shoulder circles forward and back.
5. Hands big circles forward, then back.
6. Right hand up, left down, switch hand positions with every step.
7. Bend forward and touch front foot with every step.
8. Touch opposite foot with every step.
9. Slow jogging.
10. Side step with right then left shoulder forward.
11. Jogging almost in place with High knees.
12. Jogging almost in place with High Heels.
13. Torso rotations right and left.
14. Stretch fingers, hands, shoulders
15. Stretch Leg muscles
16. Footwork
    i)   advances slow then fast
    ii) retreats slow then fast
    iii) lunge, slowly increasing in speed and range
    iv) combinations such as:
        (1) advance lunge
        (2) ballestra advance lunge
        (3) advance, appel, jump back, advance, lunge.
        (4) double retreat, advance, lunge
17. Get dressed for fencing, fence warm-up starting slowly, gradually increasing in speed. Keep in mind you are not trying to win yet. This is just warm up.

Rituals

Rituals help conquer the fear. Pump yourself up. Ritualistic dances were used by tribes to set warriors in the fighting mood.

We don't suggest humming and dancing in circles on the strip, but something more subtle is appropriate.

Frequently people are most anxious, right before they need to do something.

Let's imagine you have to parachute out of a plane for the first time. You are very scared, but you will only jump when you are good and ready.

If you come En Garde when you are nervous, referee will call fence before you take hold of your emotions and you are likely to lose. Get your emotions under control before you get to En Garde.

En Garde ritual:

Slow deep breaths in through your nose, short pause, let it out through your mouth, short pause. Breath normal. Put your front foot against the En Garde line. Move your back foot into a comfortable position. Slow deep breath in through your nose, short pause, let it out through your mouth, short pause. Breath normal. Bend your knees, raise your weapon only when completely ready.

Lost Point ritual:

Don't rush back after you lose a point. Break the rhythm, walk towards back of the strip, fix your glove, straighten your weapon. Don't focus on breaking the rhythm, focus on the strategy for your next point.

Need a break rituals:

Fencers are not allowed to take time to rest during the bout, however with permission of the referee they are allowed to take a little bit of time to fix and adjust things like:
- Fix hair.
- Fix lining of the mask.
- Pull up socks
- Straighten the weapon.
- Tie shoe laces tighter.

This is not going to buy you a lot of time, but it may be enough to catch a breath and re-focus.

Visualization

Children learn by imitating actions of adults. They see body movement and try to repeat it, with help of a more experienced individual they perfect it. When you simply imagine doing something, your brain activates many of the neural networks and cell connections as if you actually did it. If you frequently imagine performing a task, you condition your neural pathways so that the task seems familiar when you actually do it. This trains the brain and forms sinops connections. Visualize every step of the task, every small detail. This

also keeps focus away from fear. There are numerous visualization techniques specifically designed to deal with fear.

Bunny turns dragon, dragon turns bunny

Often when two evenly matched competitors meet one always wins and another loses. Loser then becomes a bunny and winner becomes a dragon.

Too many kids lose before the competition even begins. They look at who is present and make their mind up based on thinking "I always lose to him/her, this kid is so good, a winner of the last tournament..." in doing so they become a bunny.

On the other side of the room dragon is growing more confident by saying "I always win against those kids".

It is important to reinforce bunnies, encourage them and emphasize every success against their dragons, even if this success belongs to someone else. Let's say the dragon lost to another that kid bunny once beat.

Nobody is unbeatable

At the same time it is important for the dragon not to underestimate bunny. Bunny has been practicing, the tables can turn and the dragon will become a bunny.

PARENTAL CAUTION! Unless you fence yourself kids will not take your advice seriously. Wealth of knowledge you have accumulated is important, but ineffective when you are not or perceived by your kid as not a fencing expert. Don't let them to offend you and don't take offence. You are part of the team, not just a driver. Let them know that you hold their side and support them like no one else.

Roadmap

American Fencing Alliance has developed a skills chart to serve as the goal-oriented roadmap for young fencers. It clearly marks a path of learning, timing and perfecting of particular skills.

Fencer must learn and demonstrate proficiency in the following areas:
1. Footwork
2. Bladework
3. Etiquette
4. Rulles
5. Practical application of 1, 2, 3, 4 in a bout

Skills Scale by Level:
1. Knows the concept (10%)
2. Knows and understands the concept (20%)
3. Able to execute rarely (30%)
4. Able to execute sometimes (40%)
5. Able to execute 50% of the times
6. Able to execute often (60%0
7. Able to execute very often (70%)
8. Able to execute most of the times (80%)
9. Able to execute most of the times with confidence (90%)
10. Able to execute nearly flawlessly (100%)

This envisioned a four year program. The exact duration will depend on each individual's involvement and ability.

Year 1 (Month 0 - 10)
Year 2 (Month 12 - 20)
Year 3 (Month 22 - 30)
Year 4 (Month 30 - 36)

First Year

Month	Classification	Saber Skills	Passing
2	Apprentice	Advance, Retreat, Double A/R, Lunge	80%
		En Garde position, Pery 3, 4, 5 (or any 3 perries)	50%
		Fence 1-5 touch bout, knowledge of bout rules and etiquette	70%
4	Basic I	Advance, Retreat, Double A/R, Lunge, Apel Lunge,	80%
		Quick Attack, Fake Attack	50%
		En Garde position, Pery 3, 4, 5 (or any 3 perries)	70%
		Fence 1-5 touch bout, knowledge of bout rules and etiquette	80%
6	Basic II	Advance, Retreat, Double A/R, Lunge, Apel Lunge,	80%
		Quick Attack, Fake Attack	60%
		En Garde position, Pery 3, 4, 5 (or any 3 perries)	80%
		Fence 1-5 touch bout, knowledge of bout rules and etiquette	90%
8	Basic III	Advance, Retreat, Double A/R, Lunge, Apel Lunge,	80%
		Quick Attack, Fake Attack	70%
		En Garde position, Pery 3, 4, 5 (or any 3 perries)	90%
		Fence 1-5 touch bout, knowledge of bout rules and etiquette	100%
10	Musketeer I	Advance, Retreat, Double A/R, Lunge, Apel Lunge, Balestra	80%
		Quick Attack, Fake Attack, Long Attack	50%
		En Garde position, Pery 2, 3, 4, 5 (or any 4 perries)	90%
		Referee bout	30%
		Fence Pools and DE, display proper attitude	Win 1

Second Year

Month	Classification	Saber Skills	Passing
12	Musketeer II	Advance, Retreat, Double A/R, Lunge, Apel Lunge, Balestra	80%
		Quick Attack, Fake Attack, Long Attack	60%
		En Garde position, Pery 2, 3, 4, 5 (or any 4 perries)	90%
		Referee bout	30%
		Fence Pools and DE, display proper attitude	Win 1
14	Musketeer III	Advance, Retreat, Double A/R, Lunge, Apel Lunge, Balestra	80%
		Quick Attack, Fake Attack, Long Attack	70%
		En Garde position, Pery 2, 3, 4, 5 (or any 4 perries)	90%
		Referee bout	30%
		Fence Pools and DE, display proper attitude	Win 1
16	Pirate I	Advance, Retreat, Double A/R, Lunge, Apel Lunge, Balestra Lunge	80%
		Quick Attack, Fake Attack, Long Attack, Beat attack/defence	70%
		En Garde position, Pery 2, 3, 4, 5 (or any 4 perries)	100%
		Referee bout	40%
		Fence Pools and DE, display proper attitude	Win 2
18	Pirate II	Advance, Retreat, Double A/R, Lunge, Apel Lunge, Balestra Lunge	80%
		Quick Attack, Fake Attack, Long Attack, Beat attack/defence	80%
		En Garde position, Pery 2, 3, 4, 5 (or any 4 perries)	100%
		Referee bout	40%
		Fence Pools and DE, display proper attitude	Win 2
20	Pirate III	Advance, Retreat, Double A/R, Lunge, Apel Lunge, Balestra Lunge	80%
		Quick Attack, Fake Attack, Long Attack, Beat attack/defence	90%
		En Garde position, Pery 2, 3, 4, 5 (or any 4 perries)	100%
		Referee bout	40%
		Fence Pools and DE, display proper attitude	Win 2

Third Year

Month	Classification	Saber Skills	Passing
22	Duelist I	Advance, Retreat, Double A/R + L, Apel Lunge, Balestra A/L	80%
		Attack (Quick, Fake, Long), Beat attack/defence, Feints	70%
		Pery 2, 3, 4, 5, Circle 3/4 (or any 6 perries)	70%
		Advanced concepts: invitation, second intention	10%
		Referee bout	50%
		Fence Pools and DE, display proper attitude	Pass 1 Round
24	Duelist II	Advance, Retreat, Double A/R + L, Apel Lunge, Balestra A/L	80%
		Attack (Quick, Fake, Long), Beat attack/defence, Feints	80%
		Pery 2, 3, 4, 5, Circle 3/4 (or any 6 perries)	80%
		Advanced concepts: invitation, second intention	30%
		Referee bout	50%
		Fence Pools and DE, display proper attitude	Pass 1 Round
26	Duelist III	Advance, Retreat, Double A/R + L, Apel Lunge, Balestra A/L	80%
		Attack (Quick, Fake, Long), Beat attack/defence, Feints	90%
		Pery 2, 3, 4, 5, Circle 3/4 (or any 6 perries)	100%
		Advanced concepts: invitation, second intention	50%
		Referee bout	50%
		Fence Pools and DE, display proper attitude	Pass 1 Round

28	Competitor I	Advance, Retreat, Double A/R + L, Apel Lunge, Balestra A/L	90%
		Attack (Quick, Fake, Long), Beat attack/defence, Feints	80%
		Pery 2, 3, 4, 5, Circle 3/4/5 (or any 7 perries),	80%
		Advanced concepts: invitation, second intention	60%
		Referee bout	60%
		Fence Pools, DE and teams, display proper attitude	Pass 2 Rounds
30	Competitor II	Advance, Retreat, Double A/R + L, Apel Lunge, Balestra A/L	95%
		Attack (Quick, Fake, Long), Beat attack/defence, Feints	90%
		Pery 2, 3, 4, 5, Circle 3/4/5 (or any 7 perries)	80%
		Advanced concepts: invitation, second intention	70%
		Referee bout	70%
		Fence Pools, DE, teams, proper attitude, provide support to teammates	Pass 2 Rounds

Fourth Year

Month	Classification	Saber Skills	Passing
32	Competitor III	Advance, Retreat, Double A/R + L, Apel Lunge, Balestra A/L	100%
		Attack (Quick, Fake, Long), Beat attack/defence, Feints	90%
		Advanced concepts: invitation, second intention	80%
		Pery 2, 3, 4, 5, Circle 3/4/5 (or any 7 perries)	100%
		Referee bout	80%
		Fence Pools, DE, teams, proper attitude, support and organize the team	Pass 2 Rounds
34	Captain	Advance, Retreat, Double A/R, Lunge, Apel Lunge, Balestra A/L	100%
		Attacks: straight, compound, fake, feints	100%
		Defence: Beat attack/defence, Point-in-line,	100%
		Flunge, stop-cut, pris de fer	90%
		Advanced concepts: invitation, second intention	90%
		Pery 2, 3, 4, 5, Circle 3/4/5 (or any 7 perries)	100%
		Referee bout	80%
		Fence Pools, DE, teams, proper attitude, support and organize the team	Final 4 of 9 or more
36	Team Captain	Advance, Retreat, Double A/R, Lunge, Apel Lunge, Balestra A/L	100%
		Attacks: straight, compound, fake, feints	100%
		Defence: Beat attack/defence, Point-in-line,	100%
		Advanced concepts: invitation, second intention	100%
		Flunge, stop-cut, pris de fer	100%
		Pery 2, 3, 4, 5, Circle 3/4/5 (or any 7 perries)	100%
		Referee bout	90%
		Fence Pools, DE, teams, proper attitude, support and organize the team	1st of 9 or more

There is no substitute for skill.
Practice often. Practice hard.

There is not a single fencer in the world that never lost. Don't get discouraged by loses, simply practice harder. Don't expect to win and continue winning, your opponents have been practicing. Practice more, and you will become a success.

If at first you don't succeed,
Try, try, try again.

W. E. Hickson

Made in the USA
San Bernardino, CA
05 February 2020